IN
PARACHUTES
DESCENDING

PITT POETRY SERIES

TERRANCE HAYES
NANCY KRYGOWSKI
JEFFREY MCDANIEL
EDITORS

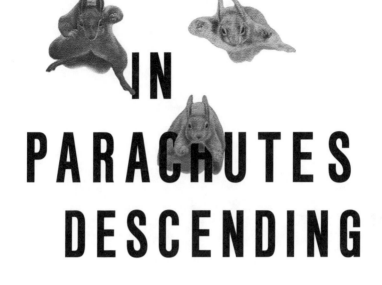

IN
PARACHUTES
DESCENDING

TANA JEAN WELCH

UNIVERSITY OF PITTSBURGH PRESS

Published by the University of Pittsburgh Press, Pittsburgh, Pa., 15260
Manufactured in the United States of America
Printed on acid-free paper
10 9 8 7 6 5 4 3 2 1

ISBN 13: 978-0-8229-6720-0
ISBN 10: 0-8229-6720-0

Cover art: Grace Mikell Ramsey, *Daughter*, 2020. Oil on canvas, 50 × 42 inches.

Cover design: Alex Wolfe

Doesn't it seem to you that the people who have the hardest time in this—this current era, whatever you want to call it . . . doesn't it seem like the people who struggle the most with it are the people who remember the old world clearly?

—Emily St. John Mandel, *Station Eleven*

Life is a generative force beneath, below, and beyond what we humans have made of it.

—Rosi Braidotti

CONTENTS

IN
PARACHUTES
DESCENDING

BOSTON UNDER WATER BY 2100

The first time
my husband and I rode our bikes
    through the Boston Harbor Hotel's arch,
        a big band on the floating stage played
            a romantic swing burdened by trombones

and even though everything went to the rent,
the grandiosity of the hotel, the rotunda, the yachts in their slips

was our grandiosity—

        we were easily drinking
     champagne while discussing
     Dean Martin's *Ten Thousand Bedrooms*

because our belief
        in love was earnest and all

we needed—

but now the stage is sinking
with the rest
of our created history:

wistful walks past Alexander Hamilton on Comm Ave,
     lavender lemonades in Copley Square,
        the Union Oyster House, our initials carved in stall 19.

Once the rain,
its tiny pressure on your scalp, like ants
                passing the door of a tobacconist.

Now the superstorm, the surging tides.

Now you and I,
        the satiated bedroom guests we never were,
        (alongside the rest of the humans) wanting
                more and more from the collapsing ground—

Now Faneuil Hall and every corner
where we met and kissed, where a thousand others met,
        conspired, or exchanged—

        each body believing
                their plot the most paramount,
                        each forgetting *history* and *story* emerged

        from the same word:

istorie—

Now and always forgetting
we build our cities to house myths,
our histories to house cities—

Soon the sea
will claim this reclaimed land,
sending these few fragments forever

to the drink. Leaving the cities, leaving
our love

to become something else.

SLEEPING WITH JANE

Last night I thought of you
while Jane slow-worked her tongue
and fingers, slow within
me an electric kistka dripping
beeswax in diamonds and spirals
on a goose egg shell.
Which isn't the same
as the way you work me
into a never-ending tocsin—
a layered alarm
sounding bomb after bomb—

Maybe I should stop
comparing lovers.

But aren't whole worlds
brought into being
by association? And separation.
As if everyone could be
Frank O'Hara. As if Boston
and San Francisco aren't two
tremendous thighs because
Harrisburg and Fresno both lack.
Waves. Bays. Paintings
by Richter and Sargent and Neel.
San Francisco is warmer,
so I live in the Mission
knowing I'd live in Pacific Heights
if I had the money.

Now Jane snores as I act
on my body alone, pressing
all that black riotous sleep
into the quiet form of daylight—
a wave on a wave—
I've collected you both. So
when Jane wakes, I kiss her
and think of you, knowing
if I were in Boston
I'd kiss you and think of her.

FIRST WINTER IN BOSTON

Dear husband,

Watching you in the dressing room mirror, face
framed by a knit cap, layering unlayering
breathable fleece and long underwear
made me think
of the first time we had sex

and of afterward:
alone in your bathroom, watching the semen
dribble from my body into the toilet
and there in the water I saw something
                                        real and tangible

something to make me believe in god,
the whole holy horde—paladins, virgins, and angels—
coming together easily
                        a miracle. This memory

then of watching you armor up in earnest
is also a memory of wanting nothing but the ache,
the wind, the lack of feeling in our toes and fingers,

and your face, always wanting your face:
a demonstration of the absolute, a blue bird in Bora Bora
protecting our bodies from the elements,
                                        swallowing the winter whole

until we weren't.

SEASTEADING: THE FINAL FRONTIER

Her lips move
      and we know what she is saying

the woman in the hot pink

skirt suit, her new blonde hair
      hired to boost

the seasteading movement:

"Floating cities are the next frontier,"

      she says and senses the host
of this cable news show about to interrupt,
      about to say something

intended to highlight her gender,
      so she rushes the next line:

"All the surface area on this planet is occupied."

      She is good

at her job so his smug jowls rest
      while she speaks
about the need for space, more space

to experiment
      with new ways of living.

But then the host reaches
  across the table, grabs
squeezes her hand in one oil slick gesture

Tell me dear,
who is allowed to live on this floating city?

her lipstick flakes as the camera
  zooms in on her face

and we can tell it wasn't the pale hand
of the host, but his question

  that woke in her eyes
an animal kingdom of jealousy

as she fears both her own exclusion

and the inclusion of all

others

in parachutes descending
upon the high seas.

STILL LIFE / TURNING LIFE

every morning Jane is amazed to find the prison island
persists—as if it were the brief petals of a poppy, a mayfly

and still   each morning the greywacke rock stands certain
so Jane wakes and paints Alcatraz, dabbing brown on

brown on blue while I pretend I'm somebody's muse

≠

why wouldn't it be there?   I ask and she answers:
"I can't help thinking this world is an Anjou pear

plucked before it's ripe."   Perhaps Jane is right
to grasp the suddenness of sinking, but her awe shouldn't

come from the dependability of islands: the incredible
thing is what she can't see from this tidy window

five miles across the bay: people clutching tour tickets
and mapping escape routes, cormorants and night herons,
blanket flowers, pansies, and tide pools

tinted by petroleum—oil tankers split open and it's all still here

in one form or another   even my body in this room
adapting to Jane and her constant turpentine smudge

≠

once—before Jane—I wanted to move to Canada or France
but then I knew:

I am leaving for another continent which is the same as this one

in which pipelines prevented from pushing through Nebraska
find another route   like my body found someone else

like the farmers in California switch to Spanish or Italian grapes
as the weather warms indefinitely: Don't fret! the viticulturalists say

become Barbera instead, or there's Negroamaro, Sangiovese,
or simply blend Albariño with your chardonnay—

trading one grape for another   without seeing
how the pieces remain scattered across the map

THE HISTORY OF THE ESCALATOR

is much like the history of space travel,
looping around on itself as one man
then another steps on the skin
of the bright combusted universe

and this is why *Playboy* used escalators
in all their ads in the 1960s
and why Wyoming has only two
escalators in the entire state—

once just a ride at Coney Island
now the sterling teeth are sharp
and inevitable as the U.S. Marine Corp
landing on islands belonging to others

because an *esca lader* is one who
escalades. So they say in the Latin:
the successful escaladers opened the gates
to the entire Persian host, the Rocky Mountains,

nuclear warfare—an astronaut's bones
rise above the atmosphere, then recede,
tapering like soda fizz, so that at night
a truce with Iran or Korea seems certain

while I am beaten to death by a thug
in a back bedroom. This is why I take
your heart and exhale the stale waste
of my last love. Why the Haitians

arriving in Miami for the first time
used to run then fall down the moving stairs,
how seemingly from nowhere
the silver steps appeared.

SEASTEADING: ENTREPRENEURIAL OPPORTUNITIES

on the sea they might sell fish
to passersby on boats
            or they might sell fish
to other like-minded people afloat

            on the floating city

the word *selfish* is seventeenth-century
Presbyterian, first used
in reference to events of the year 1641

which could be any number
of events, including but not limited to
the Iroquois declaring war against New France,
the Dutch seizure of Malacca
            (or the Dutch capture of Angola),
or the Irish Rebellion in Ulster

self-ful, *self-ended*, *self-seeking*:
synonyms used during the Early Modern era

how else to sell fish?
       freeze, pack, ship
              (no need to heed the regulations)
       string a metal needle
              through the eyes, brine
              hang dry and vacuum pack

or they might not sell it at all
but fry it on a Friday,
       swallow as much as they can

and bury the rest at sea

ORIGIN STORY (WITH FRANK O'HARA)

How it begins:
Easily. Jane said, "Meet me in the park /
if you love me." And I boarded that jet, a jade
bracelet binding paper flowers, no longer bound
to any man. For seven hours bodies
below curved and curled against
each other: hills, hills. Craters, rivers,
lake shores in lush lines. Crop circles
kissing water wheels, dunes enveloping dunes
in a soft chain across the continent. And the earth's
pliable sinuosity where the plane landed:
I went straight to Golden Gate Park and sat
near the Japanese Tea Garden, the pagodas
a perfect backdrop for her entrance.

∞

How it was:
An afternoon, all of us crafting our art.
I said to my husband: "Meet me in the park /
if you love me." And he did. Same as always:
bandstand, mouth full of tombstones,
a jagged granite smile, ghosts of martyred Quakers
skimming the Frog Pond. The Boston Common
was very common. But still, there's something
to be said for Galatea and Acis's eternal love spitting
from Brewer Fountain. Even if Acis
was crushed by a boulder in the end.
I said *meet me* and he did.

∞

How it is:
In one of the cities I walk
past the Dairy Bar and the public library,
its seven windows awash in obsoletion
and paper fliers. Then into Maurice's
Fine Chocolates to buy a balsamic
for Timothy, a Mexican spice for Kara.
Out front I spy a sparrow importing
toxins from one neighborhood
to the next—wire, skin, metallic stems. A paper
scrap, and scrawled across its dirty creases:
"Meet me in the park / if you love me."
Suddenly   we were millions
upon millions breathing this air
but not a one of us could answer
which park? what kind of love?

∞

How it begins:
Frank O'Hara listens to Prokofiev surrounded
by sheets of paper, tea cups, and Scotch
in Norman Bluhm's studio on Park Avenue South.
On one of the sheets Bluhm splats black, illustrating
the opening theme's pizzicato strings. But the poet writes
through this splashy gesture: "meet me in the park /
if you love me." Again the painter blots black
across a sheet of paper. The poet writes "apples /
light / fires / dances." Point and counterpoint,
each moves in their own medium. Paper after paper
tacked on the studio walls, the poet prints
through the paint "this is the first person / I ever
went to bed / with." The painter smears gouache over
"Help! I am alive!" and twenty-six sheets later
the sonata stops. The two men look
out the window, down to the park below,
and no one is coming.

FRANK O'HARA IS TRENDING

alongside Russia, male rompers,
summer sausage, and Jon Snow

alongside culottes
and kimono trench coats

the evidence is everywhere—

in dish towel designs
and Don Draper's last cigarette

in titles
of British novels by women named Emma

in Iceland where painters
recite his poems in former fishing plants

to trend:
to have David Bowie place you in his must-read list
to turn or roll oneself about

to spin infinitely
to make a circuit

LETTER TO THOSE WHO WANTED ME

to choose truth over dare. Self-disclose
for once. Give anything, a barbed fluke, a chain

tongue of a buckle, enough for them to claim,
I know her. She is mine.

Me. Always opting to kiss the cis girl, never holding
fast. Tagging her lips as if a hot pot, hardly

a blink. Just enough to satisfy the dare, the boy
forever asking me to strip and streak even

though my deft undress-dress celerity—perfected
in junior high locker rooms—long ago evolved

into a moonlit self-evasion, polished in pretense.

But no one wants to be left suffocating
in the polluted orchards of this valley: the earth everywhere

brown and aching. So, older now, I long
to unmoor myself, disassemble my semblance,

to imagine I never left Jess Johnson's game room
without answering questions about ejaculations,

virginity mislaid, sexual partners, and other regrets.
I would've told you I'd never fake an orgasm.

I would've shared the stale story about the back seat
of somebody's mother's Camry. Spectators

sneering round the windows. I would've told you
how many sexual partners: enough,

and the only celebrity crush I've ever had—
Frank O'Hara. Odd, but true. Because starseeds,

because a brittle desire
to land. Because Alice Neel painted his portrait

not once but twice. Because the body
is a place in which the city squats and tarries.

Because I've never faked an orgasm—
except when drunk. I would've told you

I should but don't
regret trying to OD on my mother's heart pills

at age 16. I slept five days straight and it was absolutely
fabulous. I would've said *Frank O'Hara*. Because

he "had so much grace, that man,
even through all the delirium and agony." Because sex

is a common denominator. Because humans
do things like release all the British birds

cited in Shakespeare into Central Park. Because you wanted
the truth is I would've liked to kiss her harder. Longer.

To splay myself agape. To open in slow motion
everything a body has to offer. Hers. Mine.

Middled bare in the coed dare circle—a cadaver peeled
and pinned—authenticating the thrust and gut inside us all.

THE HISTORY OF HUMANITY

while drought damages
acres of asparagus, almonds, and oranges

while a teenage boy stashes
            the strangled next-door girl

in a recycling bin, small under stacks
of corrugated cardboard bearing the black

Amazon smile, while a dentist
            from Minnesota pays $50,000
                        for the privilege of killing

a lion   fires spread

through Napa's vineyards, high-speed
trains pick off Sudanese migrants

                                    night after night—

this is why I accept your torch
moving through dangerous air

why I had three orgasms
            as southern Alaska had 21 earthquakes—

instead of asking when
the hard choices will be made

I take the torpor of touch, I feed and pulse
on the spasm of space and time

      until that generous juncture
of black hole departure—

with every climax, I can leave this world

      even as the earth's tremors deepen
by miles, even as pink iguanas live

      on the precipice of extinction
even as lightning pulls us

      farther and farther apart

LOVE (& THE HUSBAND LEFT BEHIND)

Jane never mentions you, never
says your name so it seems
you are the lost
languages Mohegan or Pochutec—

but under erasure: you expand

      to a seed, a sapling, a national park.

Like anyone scanning eBay
for the past
             I start to covet your wrist
your neck and in the dark a faint lust
stirs like a plant in the creased rain—

I want to say
there was nothing wrong
with you or us or me but Jane
grabbed my wrist one night

           and the boulder,
loosened by recent rains, tumbled down Telegraph
smashing a simple sedan parked on Lombard.

No one died

but doesn't the empty chair signify?
Become odorous with swollen longing?
A lack filled
              with another gap

until today

as if she were licking a stamp,
Jane sipped her coffee and said, "Didn't your husband
grow up in Portola?"

SLEEPING WITH JANE

Again I mutate as we move through
the old park, ready to launch
past the spectral-fired flowers,
past the Japanese elm sighing
alongside the swarm of Jizo statues,
bald little monks tall as wine bottles,
each transmitting a silent symphony
of grief—Jizo, protector of unborn babies.
Jizo, an army of stone guardians
stalwart in cardinal colored caps
and bibs—I rise above the remains

of my never known, not a phoenix
but a woman without memory, not
a man on his endless knee to the night
but a woman with a woman living in one
minute you undressed me and led me
into the pond and despite the angst of algae
between my toes I knew I was safe, like
a child who lives no longer, a child smuggled
into the afterlife in the sleeves of Jizo's robe.

IN WHICH I IMAGINE MY HUSBAND INTERVIEWED BY BARBARA WALTERS

I'll start with an easy question. What kind of tree are you?
I should want to be a sequoia—stalwart. Wide and wisened. A grip on the ground. I'd know people then, what they were capable of, their centuries of scraping nails to the nub. I'd cradle their flames in my throat and flourish. But I am likely a Japanese Maple. Called *momiji* in Japan: *baby's hands*. Songbirds eat my seeds in spring. My samaras red and ripen in early autumn, taking flight with tissue paper wings. My leaves are a beautiful fading fire. My roots are non-invasive. I won't push you out of your happy home, though you may fall.

Do you regret bringing Jane into your house, so-to-speak?
I brought my wife to the "Reclamation \ ‚re-klə-'mā-shən" exhibit at Gallery NAGA. *Reclamation*: the process of claiming something back or reasserting a right. Women reclaiming women. Jane was one of the featured artists. Sexy women painting sexy women—it was a fantastic show. They served small mu shu tacos and little Italian tuna tacos. I brought her to the gallery, but she's the one who invited Jane over and into our lives. Or perhaps Jane invited herself. It was a very sensual evening.

Were you also attracted to Jane?
She was exotic. And maybe I wanted to believe we were exotic, too. Maybe we were. Like small tigers licking each other's paws; or lashing prey, sharp tongues stripping off fur and skin and meat right to the bone. Barbed together in our lonely dynasty.

When was the last time you spoke to your estranged wife?
Christmas in Fresno, two years past. The fog was thick and we stayed at
my mother's, eating popcorn in our pajamas on the living room floor,
watching the movies families watch. Fresno is easy, time stops, especially
around the holidays. You can look out the window and see for yourself that
nothing is truly happening. So it felt good, like we were kids, someone else
was in charge and all we had to do was look to the TV and connect our
limbs into cinder. I knew about Jane by then, and the inevitability of her
leaving, but for that moment . . . my mother said we looked happy.

Did you and your wife ever consider having children?
More than 119 species practice infanticide. Males may kill to give the mother
more time for mating. But wolves. All the wolves in a pack take care of the
pups. Neither of us were raised in a pack.

And Jane?
Jane? Who knows? She was probably raised by mermaids. Flesh eating
mermaids. Perhaps she sold her soul for legs. Or for art.

What if she were to come back home? Your wife?
If she returned she'd be greeted by Arnot and five puggles howling for love. I
still live in the South End though, a studio on Tremont. I'm seeing someone.
But everything is tentative in this world. Wouldn't you say? The White
House erases "catastrophe" from the written testimony and what's melting
freezes once again.

Do you still love her? Even if she were no longer beautiful?
You asked Bo Derek this same question. I remember. I was very into Bo
Derek as a child. You asked her if she thought John would still love her if she
wasn't beautiful. Right in front of John! And Bo looked at John and said,
"That's a very difficult question."

Who am *I* to look at in response? My wife is not here.

But if she were?
I would say the moon is rising I am always thinking of the moon rising. I am
always thinking of you and because this cloud tangles itself in the black lines,
becoming spindrift and ambergris, the sea is beautiful.

HIGHWAY 99: JANE VISITS MY VALLEY

tiny teeth marks   gnashing a hole
in a paper fan purchased at the Fresno Fair

boys in the cul-de-sac shooting
rubber bands and rocks from PVC pipe guns

                this is how I remember my childhood:
                a ravenous static   a static explosion

killer sharks   floating belly up
in the sun-bleached fiberglass pool   blood
on the slide   the wasp whipping

the back of a knee   the smell
of a rattlesnake stripped of its skin
the metal barrette   the light socket

                when Jane was in the bathroom
                and my mother told me to leave Jane,
                go back to the husband in Boston
                because "You are not a lesbian"   I didn't

remind my mother of her own infidelity:
the mother-daughter "shopping trips"
to meet her lovers in San Francisco

I didn't say: "I never said I was a lesbian"

      there was only rubble, Jane bending
      to pick out a scrap of painted shirt as if
      it were soiled ivory

from a grand piano, possessed
of us both, and ruined now

in both body and skill. So that I dropped a note inviting Danny Shubin
to the Sadie Hawkins dance and later, after the school gym, found myself
pulling his hard cock on top of a guest house out in the country. On the roof
of a smaller house next to a big house next to the other big houses next to the
golf club. Weeks before

I asked and he said yes! So with money my mother didn't have, I bought
matching outfits: Vans, plaid flannel shorts, and Stüssy sweatshirts. Classic
middle California. Valley-locked

in surf-style clothes I found myself pulling his hard cock on an outdoor
chaise on top of the guest house, or maybe, the pool house. A boy and a girl
who'd exchanged less than three words in their entire lives because I was a
girl whose mother did not teach her

to speak. So I pulled and pulled at what I didn't know. I only knew his body
was tan water polo muscle and *his* mother's photo hung in the school's main
office. She died four years ago. Danny at twelve. I pulled

like the river pulls the body dumped, pulls it toward the sodden mouth.
And like the body I obeyed the current, believing the pulling was the point
in and of itself. Until he said: "I'm about to come—what are you going to
do?" Having no knowledge of *come* as naked intransitive, bare infinitive, an
infinite end we'd not yet breached

I jumped up and off the chaise, taking my hand with me. "I don't know."
Because I did not

and he did not drive me home that night or answer my calls—Danny Shubin,
ghosting before ghosting—so I learned I would never be as luminous as a
man o' war, as catching as a cage dancer. Never the one you want

SEASTEADING: RECRUITING

Seasteading.org:
Seasteading means building floating societies with significant political autonomy. "We've had the agricultural revolution, the commercial and industrial revolutions, but why not a governance revolution? Enter the sea."

Interested? Please complete this survey:

Why would you choose to live on a seastead?
(click all that apply)

- ☐ Opportunity to experiment with new governance
- ☐ Preference for small communities
- ☐ Solitude
- ☐ Love of the sea
- ☐ Desire to pioneer a new way of life
- ☐ Commercial advantages of conducting an offshore enterprise

Would you want to operate a business from the seastead?

If yes, what kind of business would you like to operate?

Do you own more than one home?

What is the total value of your real estate assets?

Do you own a timeshare?

If you own a timeshare, how much do you pay for it annually?

Do you have plenty of money?

Do you believe in Herbert Spencer?

JANE COMPLAINS

about losing wall space to Zina and Heike,
she wants a new glory hole, maybe something on Post Street—

when she's angry her voice is clanging
bangles over a thin arm, so I hear *new glory hole* instead
of *new gallery* and wonder if it's mine or hers
that's suddenly inadequate

but before the wrinkled page of the sky
swells with emptiness,
I decide to let her know:

things can always go differently

Emma Bee Bernstein committed suicide
inside the Peggy Guggenheim Collection on the Grand Canal.
She was 23.

Where did she do it?
In front of Léger's *Men in the City*
(purchased by Peggy the day Hitler invaded Normandy),
or next to Brancusi's *Bird in Space*
(acquired as the Germans approached Paris),
or in the garden? Was Emma Bee
standing on the gravesite of Peggy's 14 beloved Lhasa Apsos?

And how?

           I can't find this information anywhere.

Jane asks: what does this have to do with anything?

everything (the last dog died in 1979)

and nothing (her name was Cellida)

DE HUMANI CORPORIS FABRICA

It's the season of sun and Jane has taken to painting pictures of women in bathtubs. Women soaking with lemon slices, cucumbers, peaches. Women holding cupcakes just above the surface. She says it's from memory but they don't look like me or mine so who is she remembering? The aerial vantage: half submerged breasts, lips beneath a thin coat of gossamer blue. A slight ripple. Was Jane strapped to a ceiling? Looking down on a vintage tub, a woman, a prop: tea cup, strawberry, cheese and toast? A kind of anatomical theater?

Jane's women—thighs cradling a lotus of hair—promise perfect enlightenment.

She wants us to understand the manner of bodies. Tulip, matrix, seed and pulp: the various ways to exist. But I am not a painter, I am a poet so I only want to know: Did Jane kiss those thighs, bite those nipples? Does Buddhahood really reside in the vulva? And who are these women? Did Jane come to them covertly at night? The way Vesalius acquired his fleshy subjects to dissect? Robbing graves, waiting at the gallows for the dropped body of a pregnant woman convicted of love and heresy, or the bodies secured by his students— the ones discarded, like the torso that was once a priest's mistress. Vesalius cut them open, showing us all the ways to be a body. Ovary, uterus, cervix. Latin for scabbard: *vulva*, a sheath for holding a sword.

ALONE BUT NOT ALONE

your body is Hart Island,
floating east of the Bronx

an island dug into

filled and unfilled
by those known and unknown—

the body is a cemetery
for the forgotten and never born

a prison, a school for wayward boys
a place where every other body   lingers

like a groan from a tree
whose needles are tired of howling

so my body is yours   to touch   take
manipulate until the ferry ushers you

back to the mainland
away from the stillborn babies

the offal of desire
and whatever else the world has stuffed

inside of you   of me:

limb drop   strand of hair   orange peel
pollen   scratch and thumb print,

deadly hoof print   alone but not

EVERY BRITTLE STAR

Walking on Stinson Beach we saw one   then
      another happy yellow duck bobbing in the waves
      and the suddenness of seeing

      rubber toys gather on the winter
coast alone clipped my heart until Jane laughed
at the dozens more determined to come ashore.

Better than gym shoes she said, and began her feed of photos
      as she spoke about the thousands of Air Jordans
      riding the Pacific gyre in 1990,

      washing up in Washington and Oregon,
the separated pairs matched at swap meets—

They were gifts, Jane said, suddenly quoting O'Hara:

      these interplanetary driftings   become simple initiatory gifts
      like the circumcision of a black horse.

A storm pitched a container of Nikes into the texas tea
      dark sea—the right-feet took the Alaska Current
      to La Push and Pacific Rim, and the left-feet

      cruised the California Current to Oregon—

did they want to be separate and drifting?
      for more than 200 days

with other embryonic gifts: a salty elegance branching us to Japan,
Indonesia, Sri Lanka

in loving tsunamic arms—

Awa's laundry detergent

a soccer ball   a mannequin head

egg cartons   Styrofoam noodle cup

packing peanuts   a   toothbrush

a foam dragon sculpture

radioactive isotopes

Aromakifi shampoo

part of a *torii*, a temple gate

my faith is your faith

～

The desire to be separate and drifting is just that,
so some gifts arrive in six years, some in three
while some stay in orbit
            becoming part of the gyre's *veteris vestigial*,
it's retentive subconscious
like the memory of a moment you can't recall but remains
like a scrape in the back of the throat
            or a forgotten plum pit lodged
in the esophagus making it harder and harder to move
through the city, the neighborhood, the house.

The gyre's memory is all the stuff that we've forgotten.

The sweltering stink of what never leaves,
even what we no longer see:
stuck pill bottle   stuck seahorse lighter
stuck IUD   stuck plastic cowboy
stuck plastic Indian   stuck heart
stuck toy gun   stuck Ken and Barbie
            stuck wedding favors
stuck micro pellets that once smoothed
and sloughed the surface of your skin

And thus, *objects around us are durable, glow*
    relentlessly as if they're actually immortal.

  ~

Jane was laughing again. Thinking about the money made
    matching Nikes, the oil paint she purchased

      but not the gyres and all they contain—

garbage patches
    that photodegrade into smaller and smaller
      pieces and smaller until it becomes small

      enough for ingestion for entry into the chain
of eating of jellyfish of turtles of sharks
small fish eaten by big fish eaten by black-footed albatross or

by us—all of us, our several bodies swirling together—
    with the toxins disrupting our hormones so that one-third
    of all baby albatross die—

  ~

We are the laziest lovers

because the commercials tell us we don't need to change,
        just apologize with roses or diamonds or
        recycled bags and fuel efficiency

we place our plastic bottle on the pier

(while stopping to tie our shoe or take a photo),
allowing the wind to embrace the bottle
into the salt of the sea where it rides
the California Current south toward Mexico
where it catches the North Equatorial Current
crossing to Japan and kissing further
on the powerful Kuroshiro Current finally
lapping westward on the North Pacific Current
where the gently rolling vortexes
of the Eastern and Western Garbage Patches
gradually draw in the bottle
like the falconer hallooing his hawk

and we realize how thirsty we are.

∼

life in a gyre, our life in a gyre

used to be more or less constant, dependable   we fell
in and out of love and finally felt nothing

                              but now, this undependable

          alternate universe

                         where logic falters

and it snows in Hawaii   and I find myself kissing

a woman and the Arctic's Beaufort Gyre has refused
to turn counterclockwise as it should

                    every five to seven years—

                                   stuck since 1997,

                                        the gyre isn't widening,

                                             it's leaking

freshwater into the Atlantic Ocean—disrupting

the ocean conveyor system, disrupting the climate

so the lapping waves lap louder, higher, a syncopated osculation of

what's happening over there

is always happening over here

∼

These several bodies swirling into breath, movement, sea
turtles swimming from Japan to Baja, eels
hitching to Greenland and Maine, always going

somewhere before wrapped around a rice roll
(your legs around me, mine around Jane)
and there is bacteria, minerals, microbials,

flotsam and jetsam, drift and debris
because there are cargo ships and storms, there are a slew
of rubber duckies floating in the Pacific alongside 32,000 pieces

of hockey gear—gloves, guards, and pads—alongside
Legos and computer chips, alongside the human
animalness of every private heart, every brittle star—

OCTOBER RENGA

—with Frank O'Hara

A single raspberry
floats in a flute
of Soligo Prosecco.

Mournful glass, and daisies
closing. Hay swells in the nostrils.

I find the scars
on her arms at once hard
to love and not love.

Beside the sea, green mammoths
with frothing lips, the long razor

scraping shale. The wind
turbine's heavy blade clips
a griffon vulture in Crete.

Blackness under the trees, stone
walls, smelling faintly of semen.

In this field where things
happen: find a pair of panties,
find two copper pennies.

It's next to my flesh,
that's why. I do what I want.

JANE AT TWELVE

She eats *crêpes* and *croque-madames* and escapes her mother as much as possible, sitting most days at *La Perle*, pretending to smoke. She absolutely objects to Euro Disney but agrees to see Metallica at the Hippodrome because she is secretly hoping for a riot like the one in Montreal. She wants to see impulse embodied. To see if it's as she expects: a beautifully choreographed affair of long-limbed girls outrunning the floods, flying war planes, pulling the world's last thread. There was no riot, but the first song played was "Creeping Death" and the last "So What" and Jane cannot help but think this says something about her own evolving status.

And now she has lost her mother again as she sits on a train to Auvers-sur-Oise. An unaccompanied minor daytripping to her dream shrine, a tangible tank top, the espresso bitter, her breasts hard and she is in love with Van Gogh as all young girls are, their dripping hearts split over who is the best mind of every generation—Vincent or Sylvia? And this has not been the summer of shirtless boys burning cars she thought it would be, rather, like a whip made from the sheerest stockings, Paris has been what her mother said—a sensible way to forget her father.

The train passes through Saint-Denis and the woman across from her notices a copy of Collette's *Earthly Paradise* next to Jane's thigh. "Ah," says the woman, "Does the dove fancy herself *une jeune gousse*?" Jane smiles like someone conceding her desire to be *matériel de masturbation* for every man and woman on this continent and the next. Although the book was there well before she sat down, she never makes it to the church at Auvers. Never sees reality rendered through Van Gogh's violet violence. But still, because Jane is Jane, she is not late for the curtain as the theater explodes in a sheet of flame which is her breathing always.

THE REAL NIGHTMARE

When pressed

      by new and old strangers
on why I left my husband, I always
tell the truth:
          we devoured each other

hungry for toes and tits, a salt lick
of limbs   orgasm after orgasm
until it felt like the whole world
      was coming

to nothing
but splinters of the driest branch.

I know this is a classic story because
it shuts them up.

But now
if I turn down my sheets
children start screaming
through windows   and Jane shakes
     me awake, asking

if it was the city or the valley
     nightmare. Her hand a dynasty

of emerald hummingbirds
saving us all from famine,

from the real nightmare:

that I'll gobble Jane too, act
as a wendigo slurping her body
to the nub—

or is this the truly bad dream:
that the appetite was never there?

Safety the only thing to savor.

SEASTEADING: EPHEMERISLE

Ephemerisle is a floating celebration
      of community and seasteading.

There are no tickets, no central organizers,
      and no rangers to keep you safe.

      Ephemerisle prepares us
for our future world through five days
      of floating

      on the Sacramento River Delta.

You must practice radical self-reliance.
      You must build a boat.
There is limited space. There are no rangers
to keep you safe.

You are free to do what you want.
You must conform to the island commodore's rules.
      There are no rangers to keep you safe.

You are free to do what you want.
      You can sleep in the nude.
You can eat all of your food.
You can carve trees in your calves
      with a switchblade or machete.

You can hoard life jackets and flares.
You can snort several lines of pure white Prague.
You can keep your drawbridge raised.

You can hoist a flag
depicting buckteeth biting watermelon,
        but there are no rangers to keep you safe.
You can dress your feet in pink FiveFingers.
You can have ten wives

        and your way
            with their daughters (and sons).

You *can* not give a shit. You can sink your boat.

NO ONE SHOULD FEEL THAT ALONE

Jane was handing someone a bouquet of satay,
gushing about Muller's Foreign Cinema and Laszlo,
when I told her about the abortion. A party

not the best place to breathe new disclosures, to say:
The baby would be three years old now.

I moved to a conversation about metal maps
and the cosmic center of Himalayan Buddhism,
but at home Jane wanted to know all about it, the belly

of black sky, the ghost baby that crashed her friend's gala.
By then I could only speak in negatives, only walk through

what never happened. The leafy plants were red
and Jane's blue gown was the color of flaming poppies
and I didn't want to keep it. And I didn't

arrive at the clinic with a teenage boy who said,
"We drove all this way. Stop crying; act like a woman."

The closest clinic wasn't 300 miles away.
I took the subway. I didn't tell my husband. I didn't take a pill.
I didn't shit or vomit. My hand was sweaty

and the speculum was icy, but there wasn't a tiny
poster of a tropical island pasted on the ceiling.

I don't know how I came up with $700. The doctor didn't whistle
"Without Love" or "Springtime for Hitler" while vacuuming
my uterus, but I still shudder whenever I hear show tunes.

The technician didn't tell me how large the head was—
not a walnut, lemon, avocado, or ripened plum.

I didn't have a boyfriend who wanted sex
afterward, even when I said "No, it still hurts." Or
a husband waiting in the waiting room,

a husband asking, "Where do you want to go on vacation?"
Perhaps try the dry white wines of the Mediterranean coast?

When it was over, a nurse didn't say,
"It was a shad a snake a sparrow and a boy's closed eye."
At dinner we didn't say let's have her and at breakfast: no.

More monster than murdered, safe in all silences.
Oh dear Jane do you want to know I was covered in blood?

Do you want to know about the tiny bright room?
The women who were afraid? The girls who smiled?

MISSION DISTRICT MURAL #63: ¡VIVA LA TAMALE LADY!

Tamale Lady (2013)

Artists: Megan Wilson, Jet Martinez
Location: Clarion Alley, Mission
Current State: Not available (painted over)

I.

Now you're a citizen
you must eat tamales, Jane exclaimed
during my first September

in San Francisco, beginning what became better
known as the month spent drinking
amore veitatos, bloody marys, or just gin.

We traversed the constellation of local bars
in search of the patron saint of city drunks,
everyone's surrogate abuelita,

and finally, on the twenty-seventh night,
The Tamale Lady appeared at the Zeitgeist
looking every bit the lush Madonna

wearing a t-shirt that read, *you don't know me
but I love you*, lugging a Coleman cooler loaded
with trash bags full of homemade tamales.

We devoured her morsels of meat tucked
in sweet masa, proclaiming they were as good
as everyone said, because if they weren't,

then the month was a loss. A firestorm
to the liver. Nothing more than a September
of sloppy sex, hangovers, and unfinished art.

II.

Frank O'Hara once said, "To lie flat
on the earth in spring, summer, or winter is sexy,"
and I've always agreed. Which is telling:

I am the laziest lover. Which is telling: Jane
was so attractive because she did the work
so well   like fingers stringing a star

and all I had to do was lie
and breathe her anesthesia, dream
of rapture, the tongue of an exotic tiger.

III.

Now after 20 years of service, the tamale lady
has been banned from selling in bars—
a public health violation, a lack of license. Now

after 3 years of service, Jane is tired
of my lying about. Or, she sees other women.
Or perhaps, I too, never had the license

to transact. Jane, Supervisor Campos, and the *Mission
Local* all say not to worry, the city plans to help
Ms. Ramos open a lawful operation.

Some say a criminal shouldn't receive such assistance.
Some say ¡*Viva la tamale lady*! While others say *I'm white!
What about me?* And then there are those who say

she is an institution and we must keep our institutions.
Our essence, form, and order. But is this true desire?
The tamales were only good because *they came to us,*

to our hands and mouths when we needed them most.

EXPECT ANY ANSWER

Frank O'Hara was a ram

born hot but he died
        believing he was a Cancer, a crab clacking
                in his own strong water. If he knew

his life began in March instead of June,
would he have been so devastated by any death?

Would he have given up sex with strangers in 1957?

Would he still have fell to his knees
        at the feet of Giulietta Masina, Fellini's *Lo Spippolo*,
                another small thing pushing O'Hara

toward tenderness? Does he still suffer
        from the stale enervation of waking to bourbon
                and orange juice? Would an Aries nurse

James Schuyler through episodes of schizophrenia, hiding
        him in the Hamptons, wiping his million terrors—
                the encroaching fog, babies, sulphur

and tulips—from public view? Or send a telegram
        to Boris Pasternack applauding his Nobel win?

Perhaps this is like asking

if Russia hadn't refused Pasternak the Nobel Prize,
        would he still have died two years later,
                his lungs clouded with lesions?

or if Putin hadn't jailed Pussy Riot
        would we still need John Kerry to slap his wrist
                with a ruler every third day?

At the end of a three-hour sit down with said dictator,
        Madeline Albright described Putin as "so cold
                as to be almost reptilian"—

                                Perhaps he'd agree

we are only ever who we think we are.

Sensitive or strong, humane or hungry, the one never caught,
        never given up for dead. The one always wearing pink or red.

Stalin said it was going to be a long game.

And when I ask myself,
                if I would've stayed in bed
or Boston would I not now be living with this lavender kimono-
sized loneliness? I cannot expect any answer other than yes
        or no.

"JESUS DIED ON THE CROSS BECAUSE HE FORGOT HIS SAFE WORD"

read the sign
at the Hunky Jesus Contest
that Easter Sunday in Golden Gate Park

where Jesus after Jesus performed his passion—

twerked to "Shake that Monkey,"
erected nipples in milk spray,
bore his burden in fishnets and high heels,
drained cabernet from his biceps—

a stage full of Jesuses who mostly looked
like they'd never say their safe word.

Jane was looking for someone to paint
and I was just looking. Sisters
of Perpetual Indulgence—what Jane said
we could be, what we were, together

and I liked the sound of it, a pitch better
and cooler than I knew myself to be, a sound
like a summit of ecstasies clad in leather
moto pants. A blue-limbed star whipping, but

by then I also knew
Jane, and Jane and I together, and we weren't
the same Order as the cross-dressing nuns of fun
throwing this party.
                              Yes, we were good
at drinking and eating and screwing

but I'd read their website. Being a Sister
isn't just securing wigs and corsets, but more
helping hospice and school, pushing
raffle tickets, lining up port-a-potties—

Like everything, indulgence is multiple
with meaning, including the gratification
of another. And while the Sisters served others,

Jane and I, like true Republicans, yielded only
to our own desires, like song birds singing

for territory, or goblins mating with Caligula—
so when Jane winked and said we were sisters
perpetually indulging, I knew

despite the display of Jesuses offering
remission of all my sins

what I truly learned from sleeping with Jane
was not relaxation of restraint

but that the Muse poses
only when she is bivouacked
and wants to get out,

which is what Jane and I both craved—to evade

one existence for another. But having conquered
this aura, this life of love away from love,
what next? Where do we go? Which of us
now needs a safe word and why?

SEASTEADING: MANIFEST DESTINY

the right to expand:

like a Chinese fan (bamboo and paper, feathers under a roof)
or salt water taffy (stretching from mouth to mouth)

like a uterus (the inching baby kicking)
or earth's flowing mantle (the seafloor spreading)

just like the puffer fish (large with poison)
or the cobra flaring its hood (before the venom, before the kill)

HEAT SIGNATURE

When the lockdown is lifted I imagine
not Boston but you emerging
from under the sheets, sex always
your default mode when cities are bombed.
You take her body by the hand,
tell her it's all right, all good and safe
to go to Hamersley's for spring sorbets.

Hours later alone I watch the police video,
watch the apprehension: the heat
signature of a boy bleeding in a boat,
his ultraviolet body captured infrared
as he writes his future past
on the cabin wall, writes in pencil
and blood: . . . *know you are fighting men*
who look into the barrel of your gun and see
heaven, now how can you compete with that . . .
killing innocent people is forbidden in Islam
but due to said [bullet hole] it is allowed.
All credit goes to [bullet hole].

I watch the boy bombardier
writing and swinging
inside himself a clang
like the tongue of a bell, smaller
and larger but growing
with every streaming bite.

THE HISTORY OF SUICIDE

My friend said it was unethical to write about Emma Bee Bernstein, to mention her in a poem, to name the thing the way I did—"Emma Bee Bernstein committed suicide / inside the Peggy Guggenheim collection on the Grand Canal." My friend said it was cruel. And she knows I am not cruel.

I am not cruel, but I am fascinated. And sad.

Because I visited Peggy's Venetian palazzo when I was 23 (the age Emma was when she suddenly wasn't). Because all I remember is the gravestone for those dogs. Because I remember loving it—not the gravestone but the palazzo, well, maybe the gravestone, too. (Or maybe the idea of being buried next to so many dogs.) Because when I found out Emma was an intern at Peggy's, I thought, *how lucky!* Emma gets to be (to breathe) in Venice, and *how lucky!* her mother is an artist and her father a poet. I grew up in Fresno; my mother sells insurance, my father is a cop.

Because I also thought, *Suicide in the museum! What balls!*

First I felt she did it in front of the Léger or Brancusi's bird, but now I'm burning beyond the obvious—there's Appel's crocodile trying to catch the sun (which is also somewhat obvious, what with the crying and the frenetic hand gesticulations), or Bacon's chimpanzee, a distorted human inching toward the cardinal abyss. Or perhaps she was in the climate-controlled storage space, among the crates and flats of the less than important pieces in Peggy's collection.

The word *suicide* is mentioned 5 times in Frank O'Hara's *Collected*. I don't know if that's a lot or not. In one poem, O'Hara wishes his mother the sensation of a suicide in her suburban neighborhood, and another features the dark red armory where a pianist engaged in self-slaughter. And then there are these lines from "Hôtel Transylvanie":

> for six seconds of your beautiful face I will sell the hotel and commit
> an uninteresting suicide in Louisiana where it will take them a long time
> to know who I am / why I came there / what and why I am made to happen

Emma Bee Bernstein's suicide was decidedly interesting. Still, it will take them a long time.

And how and how and how?

WHY JANE WAS BUT WASN'T REAL

Dear husband,

because I could survive death
but not the thread

habitually unraveling
because the love trailing your tongue

grew expected
like a French person speaking French

because when women say they love
having sex, they really mean

they love orgasms
because there is a difference

because no one told me my hair
or my thighs would change

like stars and their patterns, first not at all
then seemingly sudden and en masse

because you gave me such a small piece of linen
to cover my heart

because the struggle to know a body
is futile

hollow as a mass shooting, paltry
as a paper lantern lighting a windowless room

EVENTUALLY EROSION

How gone are Sammy and Lola
ticking up down
the stairwell, Puerto Rican girls
tall in summer dresses

coyly refusing to pose
for your paint palette
with a wink and a smack
so you took
to calling them Red
and Plum—the colors you dreamed
when you dreamed

in young girls. Their quick tongues
and arable bodies kept us in bed
trying hard to love

what was already leaving. You
were certain they'd come
around. But Jane

the most beautiful things in life
disappear—

like the sandstone spires
in Utah, the long curvy clay
shrinks and swells,
erodes with rain and falls
when pushed
by a troop of scouts—

these disappearances
along the shore
ripple without a quake
because all

is never and always lost:
(Sammy and Lola moved
to San Jose,) so what

the unapologetic scout master
told the Salt Lake Sentinel—

eventually erosion
brings all of them down—

was only half right.

What was already leaving: the way

I saw you:

a cosmic string,

      volcanic lightning, my own chimerical

solar flare—

          But don't worry
     sweet Jane,

eventually erosion
brings us some other place.

Even if, for a time, it feels like we are nowhere else.

NOT THIS BOSTON

Bored of my intentional
community and all
the California artists
pretending to keep bees

I went back
longing to see
the same city, walked
every sidewalk

and waited to feel
summer of '07 happy,
but Hamersly's was gone,
the South End townhouses
all belonged to the new breed
of women teaching their babies
Spanish while in Supta Konasana.

The Mother Church
and her reflecting pool
no longer reflected
an endless stream of exceptional
stars. Everything a dull
sickly tympanic membrane,

so to the North
End! I watched an armory
combing its bronze bricks,
a busker braiding fire—
but even that was cold.

Not the same
city nine years later, this Boston
of my lonely commercial ache,
this Boston of the self who forgot
the difference a body makes—
how yours makes mine
singular.

THE IMMORTAL JELLYFISH

To extend our human season
the scientist devotes himself to the scarlet jellyfish
from Wakayama Bay. We will learn

to be immortal, to rejuvenate—
and then, he says, and then
we will be better

&

so he pierces the tiny body
to create the critical crack: the trauma
needed to become something new:

he stabs then scrambles
until the frail face
stops pulsing

a parachute deflated

&

ichi, ni, san—

in three days, the battered
jelly-cum-micro-Jesus
roots down and clones itself into a band

of identical children knotted together,
a chain of polyps sleeping softly
in water-filled jars. He feeds them brine shrimp,

sings karaoke until they grow into hundreds
of new medusae, an unassuming garden
of miniscule troopers—

He never skips a day. Jellyfish and karaoke.
Jellyfish and karaoke. He never skips a day.

He does it over and over
so we can learn
to be never-ending, to regenerate
just like the *Turritopsis dohrnii*—

and then, he says, and then
we will be better
able to appreciate the wonder

of atoms and cells,
of essence and dominion.

THE IMMORTAL JELLYFISH II

Water, of course, is a must
for the regenerating jellyfish.
And if burnt—like ahi seared,
or a girl stumbling into the sea
side fire—they're no longer
everlasting. Jellies cannot rise
from the dead while residing
in a stomach—not even the shark's
spacious u-shaped paunch—
but conditions aside

does sprouting anew
always (or ever) guarantee gratitude
and wonder? Must the body be
truly new, or just new to me? The day
I smoothed my hand over the slope
of Jane's nakedness I felt revived: a Brazilian
at the beach, or just myself electrified?
The jolt of the lever, the monster

animated. And given a new body,
would we do this world any differently?

Or this: what if all bodies
perpetually rolled into a single ball
of ever-changing existence?
There is another man who believes
we can be better, with a computer
instead of a microscope, he spends days
nights dreaming of games so fun
humanity stops fighting. He eats
soba noodles and imagines a drunken bender
in which the King of All Cosmos destroys
stars and planets, leaving the tiny prince
to pick up the pieces. A video game
so fun we all stop fighting. But still
there is history—which is human
and tumbling, a *katamari damacy*,
a magical adhesive ball growing bigger
by rolling over what is smaller,
which in Japanese means "soul clump."

MASQUERADE

Because the Bengal tiger only
attacks from behind, the honey
harvesters and fishermen in
India's mangrove forests wear
a rubber mask—a pale-faced
human with a thin mustache—
on the back of the skull.

A two-faced trick more survival
than deception, like but not like
the scientists who camouflage
their visage into pandas, cranes,
and crocodiles to get closer to
the creatures they're trying to
save.

Like but not like myself, who as
a young girl dreamed of dressing
like a man so as to be a man, to
be able to do what I wanted—

to fight, wield weapons, crave
my face unmade, my hair short.
To not be a girlfriend or a wife.
To not worry about anything.
But somewhere along the way
it became harder to distinguish
between survival and deception,
between the longing to be

sheltered and different and insane and decorative as a Mayan idol too well understood to be beautiful. So I embraced the double-bind of short skirts, boosted breasts.

And I got what I wanted, but mostly I didn't.

Still, the tedious costume became a habit, the height of heels too high to surrender. And now I am with Jane, femme to her femme.

And now Kurdish women brandish AK-47s, fight ISIS, rescue mothers and daughters, while taking time to apply makeup before strapping on the rifle—mascara, shadow, lipstick—not to proclaim their freedom, but so the enemy will look at her and know he dies by the hands of a woman, know he goes straight to hell without collecting his virgins.

ISIS fighters would rather run than die this way. So this makeup, this mask, is also about survival.

As is the guise of the Japanese paantu, faces covered in muddy vines, smearing sooty muck on babies and children to thwart evil, to bring good health.

That when I mull over the many masks Jane wears, or wonder if she has counted my own, I attend the masquerade like a courtier devouring, like a dancer caught fire, I heed the transformation as resuscitation

knowing I was never so much myself as when I took on a shape made by someone else.

NOTES

The O'Hara line in "Origin Story (with Frank O'Hara)" is not from a poem but from O'Hara's artistic collaboration with painter Norman Bluhm, "Meet Me in the Park" (1960).

The quote about O'Hara in "Letter to Those Who Wanted Me" comes from Willem de Kooning and his description of O'Hara upon visiting him in the hospital the day he died. See "Frank O'Hara: He Made Things and People Sacred," originally published in *The Village Voice* on August 11, 1966.

The survey in "*Seasteading*: Recruiting" was taken from Seasteading.org in 2015; it is a word for word reproduction barring the last two questions. Since then, the Seasteading website has undergone a facelift—the work of a well-paid PR firm, perhaps—and now emphasizes "moral imperatives" over making money, evading taxes, and operating without regulation.

Printed in 1543, *De humani corporis fabrica* (*On the Structure of the Human Body*) by Andreas Vesalius was the first comprehensive textbook of human anatomy.

In addition to the line from O'Hara, "Every Brittle Star" also includes a line from Ruth Ozeki's *A Tale for the Time Being* and Erika Meitner's *Copia*.

Due to the collaborative nature of the renga, the alternating couplets in "October Renga" are all borrowed from O'Hara.

"Expect Any Answer" was inspired by a post on Andrew Epstein's blog *Locus Solus* on March 27, 2014. Epstein writes, "As Brad Gooch details in his biography of O'Hara, *City Poet*, O'Hara believed that he was born on June

27, 1926. That's what his parents told him, and presumably that was the date he always celebrated as his birthday. [...] As Gooch notes, this means that O'Hara (who called himself 'an ardent horoscope reader') wasn't even aware of his correct astrological sign. Ironically, in October 1959, he wrote a poem about being a Cancer, when he was actually an Aries."

The Hunky Jesus Contest of "Jesus Died on the Cross Because He Forgot His Safe Word" is exactly what it sounds like: may the best looking Jesus win. The Sisters of Perpetual Indulgence is a leading-edge order of queer and trans nuns who believe all people have a right to express their unique joy and beauty. Since their first appearance in San Francisco on Easter Sunday 1979, the Sisters have devoted themselves to community service, ministry, and outreach to those on the edges and to promoting human rights, respect for diversity, and spiritual enlightenment. To learn more about the Sisters, visit their website, www.thesisters.org, or their Facebook and Instagram pages. (With thanks to D. A. Powell.)

"The Immortal Jellyfish" was inspired by the Vice documentary *The Jellyfish That Holds a Key to Immortality* and the work of Shin Kubota. The video game creator in "The Immortal Jellyfish II" is Keita Takahashi.

ACKNOWLEDGMENTS

Grateful acknowledgment is made to the editors of the journals where the following poems first appeared:

Colorado Review: "Expect Any Answer," "Not This Boston," and "Letter to Those Who Wanted Me"; *Four Way Review*: "Sleeping with Jane" (2) and "Jane Complains"; *Green Mountains Review*: "No One Should Feel That Alone"; *North American Review*: "Sleeping with Jane" (1); *The Pinch*: "¡Viva La Tamale Lady!"; *Pleiades: Literature in Context*: "Seasteading" (all sections); *Prairie Schooner*: "The Real Nightmare"; *subtropics*: "Origin Story (with Frank O'Hara)"; *Sugar House Review*: "October Renga" and "Boston Under Water by 2100"; *Under a Warm Green Linden*: "The History of the Escalator," "Frank O'Hara Is Trending," and "Highway 99: Jane Visits My Valley."

"*De humani corporis fabrica*" appeared in *Bared: An Anthology on Bras and Breasts*, edited by Laura Madeline Wiseman.

With gratitude to my many entanglements: Moose, Randy, Betty, Ethan, Mary, Laura, Karen, all the Sharrocks (especially Auntie), the in-laws and out-laws, the Ladies Home Journal Club, the DFMRH, Boston, San Francisco, Tallahassee, Madison, San Diego, Clovis and Fresno.

Special thanks to Lauren Russell and Charlotte Pence for their valuable comments on manuscript drafts.

And oceans of love to my three-owl-family. My best PFD. My inherently buoyant hands-free floaty pants: Timothy and Berkeley (BOZ) Welch.